S0-BYJ-836

Rosa Parks

Published by Roaring Brook Press
Roaring Brook Press is a division of Holtzbrinck Publishing Holdings Limited Partnership
175 Fifth Avenue, New York, NY 10010
mackids.com

Library of Congress Control Number: 2017957520
ISBN 978-1-250-16617-3

Our books may be purchased in bulk for promotional, educational, or business use. Please contact your local bookseller or the Macmillan Corporate and Premium Sales Department at (800) 221-7945 ext. 5442 or by e-mail at MacmillanSpecialMarkets@macmillan.com.

First published in France in 2016 by Quelle Histoire, Paris
First U.S. edition, 2018

Text: Clémentine V. Baron
Translation: Catherine Nolan
Illustrations: Bruno Wennagel, Mathieu Ferret, Aurélie Verdon

Printed in China by RR Donnelley Asia Printing Solutions Ltd., Dongguan City, Guangdong Province

10 9 8 7 6 5 4 3 2 1

Rosa Parks

Roaring Brook Press
New York

Growing Up

Rosa Parks is called the First Lady of Civil Rights. She fought for laws that are fair to every American, no matter their skin color.

Rosa was born in Tuskegee, Alabama, on February 4, 1913. She grew up on her grandparents' farm. Rosa's mother taught her that equality for all people was important. But Rosa knew many things were not equal.

1913

Black and White

Rosa went to a school that was just for black children. There was a nicer school nearby that was just for white children.

The black students walked to school. The white students got to ride a bus.

Back then, laws kept black people and white people apart. They gave more rights to white people than black people.

The laws were foolish and unfair.

1920

Montgomery

When she was a teenager, Rosa left the farm. She moved to the city of Montgomery.

Rosa met a barber named Raymond Parks there. Raymond was an activist. He fought for equal rights for African American people.

In 1932, Raymond asked Rosa to marry him. Rosa said yes!

1927–1934

Enough Is Enough

Rosa graduated from high school. She found work as a seamstress. Rosa wanted a better job. But many companies would not hire black workers.

Rosa looked around. She saw jobs she couldn't get, restaurants she couldn't eat in, bathrooms she couldn't use—all because she was black. Rosa wasn't even allowed to vote!

Rosa had had enough. But what could she do? How could she make things change?

1934–1955

The Bus

One December day, Rosa headed home from work. She was sitting on a city bus.

A white man wanted Rosa's seat. The bus driver told Rosa she had to give her seat to him. That was the law.

Rosa said no.

She didn't know it, but this small act was the start of a big change.

December 1, 1955

Arrested

The driver warned Rosa that he would call the police. Rosa said calmly, "You may."

The police arrested Rosa. They took her to jail and kept her there for hours.

December 1, 1955

The Protest

A young minister named Martin Luther King Jr. heard about Rosa's arrest. He started a boycott. He asked black people to stop riding the bus.

Day after day, black people in Montgomery walked or biked to work. The buses stayed empty. Some bus lines lost so much money that they were shut down.

This went on for 381 days.

1955–1956

CLOSED

Victory

The boycott worked! In November 1956, the bus law changed. Now black riders had the same rights as white riders. Rosa was glad.

But the boycott was hard on Rosa. She and Raymond both lost their jobs. Their lives were threatened.

They had to leave Montgomery to stay safe.

November 13, 1956

Civil Rights Act

Rosa didn't let fear stop her. She joined Martin Luther King Jr. and other civil rights leaders. They led marches. They made speeches.

Their voices were heard. President Lyndon B. Johnson signed the Civil Rights Act in 1964. This new law struck down a lot of the old, unfair laws.

It was a huge step forward.

1964

Fifty Years

In 2005, people gathered to hear Rosa speak. It had been fifty years since she refused to give up her seat on a bus. America had changed for the better, thanks in part to Rosa.

Rosa died later that year. She and her brave bus ride will never be forgotten.

2005

50th
BUS BOYCOTT

1913
Born Rosa McCauley in Tuskegee, Alabama.

1934
Rosa finishes high school in Montgomery.

1955
The start of the bus protest.

1956
The end of the bus boycott. Black riders board buses again.

1910

1932
Rosa marries Raymond Parks.

1955
Rosa is arrested for refusing to give up her bus seat.

1956
The law changes so that black riders have the same rights as white riders on city buses.

1957
Rosa and Raymond mov
to Detroit, Michigan.

1963
Rosa joins the March on Washington for Jobs and Freedom.

1964
President Lyndon B. Johnson signs the Civil Rights Act.

1965
Rosa marches with Martin Luther King Jr. to demand voting rights.

1987
Rosa starts a school to help children learn about the civil rights movement.

1996
Rosa receives the Presidential Medal of Freedom Award from President Clinton.

2005
Rosa Parks dies in Detroit.

2010

North America
CANADA
UNITED STATES
MEXICO
1
2
3
4
5
6

MAP KEY

1 Tuskegee, Alabama

Rosa Parks was born in this small town in the southern United States.

2 Pine Level, Alabama

When Rosa was very young, her father left home to work in the north. The rest of the family lived on her grand-parents' farm in Pine Level.

3 Montgomery, Alabama

Rosa went to school and met her husband in this Alabama state capital. The city is now famous for its role in the civil rights movement.

4 Detroit, Michigan

After the Montgomery bus boycott, Rosa and Raymond moved here. They lived in Detroit for the rest of their lives.

5 Washington, DC

On August 28, 1963, over 200,000 Americans marched for civil rights through the streets of the nation's capital. Martin Luther King Jr. gave his famous speech, "I Have a Dream."

6 Selma, Alabama

In March 1965, Rosa joined Martin Luther King Jr. on a march from Selma to Mont-gomery to demand voting rights for black people.

People to Know

Raymond Parks

(1903–1977)

Rosa's husband was a barber. He fought for civil rights, just like Rosa.

Martin Luther King Jr.

(1929–1968)

He was the most famous figure in the civil rights movement. He was only thirty-nine years old when he was shot and killed.

Lyndon B. Johnson

(1908–1973)

The thirty-sixth president of the United States signed the Civil Rights Act in 1964 and the Voting Rights Act in 1965.

Edgar Daniel Nixon

(1899–1987)

He was the civil rights leader in Alabama who asked Dr. King to start the bus boycott.

Did You

KNOW?

Rosa Parks was not the first black woman to be arrested for refusing to give up her seat. Fifteen-year-old Claudette Colvin was arrested nine months earlier in Montgomery, Alabama.

Rosa Parks received the Presidential Medal of Freedom in 1996 and the Congressional Gold Medal in 1999.

Did You KNOW?

More than 30,000 people went to the U.S. Capitol to pay their respects to Rosa Parks after she died.

In 2005, many cities celebrated the anniversary of Rosa Parks's bus ride by leaving certain seats empty on city buses.

Available Now

Coming Soon